RELIGIOUS, CULTURAL, AND MINORITY RIGHTS

FOUNDATIONS OF DEMOCRACY

Citizenship and Immigration

Corruption and Transparency

Employment and Workers' Rights

Gender Equality and Identity Rights

Justice, Policing, and the Rule of Law

Political Participation and Voting Rights

Religious, Cultural, and Minority Rights

Speech, Media, and Protest

RELIGIOUS, CULTURAL, AND MINORITY RIGHTS

David H. Holt

Series Advisor: Tom Lansford
Professor of Political Science
University of Southern Mississippi, Gulf Coast

MASON CREST

Mason Crest
450 Parkway Drive, Suite D
Broomall, PA 19008
www.masoncrest.com

MTM Publishing, Inc.
435 West 23rd Street, #8C
New York, NY 10011
www.mtmpublishing.com

President: Valerie Tomaselli
Vice President, Book Development: Hilary Poole
Designer: Annemarie Redmond
Copyeditor: Peter Jaskowiak
Editorial Assistant: Andrea St. Aubin

Series ISBN: 978-1-4222-3625-3
Hardback ISBN: 978-1-4222-3632-1
E-Book ISBN: 978-1-4222-8276-2

Library of Congress Cataloging-in-Publication Data
Names: Holt, David H., 1970– author.
Title: Religious, cultural, and minority rights / by David H. Holt.
Description: Broomall, PA: Mason Crest, 2017. | Series: Foundations of
   democracy | Includes index.
Identifiers: LCCN 2016004313 | ISBN 9781422236321 (hardback) | ISBN
   9781422236253 (series) | ISBN 9781422282762 (ebook)
Subjects: LCSH: Freedom of religion—Juvenile literature. | Human rights—Juvenile
   literature. | Minorities—Civil rights—Juvenile literature.
Classification: LCC BL640 .H65 2017 | DDC 323—dc23
LC record available at https://lccn.loc.gov/2016004313

Printed and bound in the United States of America.

First printing
9 8 7 6 5 4 3 2 1

TABLE OF CONTENTS

Key Icons to Look for:

 Words to Understand: These words with their easy-to-understand definitions will increase the reader's understanding of the text, while building vocabulary skills.

 Sidebars: This boxed material within the main text allows readers to build knowledge, gain insights, explore possibilities, and broaden their perspectives by weaving together additional information to provide realistic and holistic perspectives.

 Research Projects: Readers are pointed toward areas of further inquiry connected to each chapter. Suggestions are provided for projects that encourage deeper research and analysis.

 Text-Dependent Questions: These questions send the reader back to the text for more careful attention to the evidence presented there.

 Series Glossary of Key Terms: This back-of-the-book glossary contains terminology used throughout the series. Words found here increase the reader's ability to read and comprehend higher-level books and articles in this field.

Iraqi women at a political rally in 2010, in advance of the country's parliamentary elections.

SERIES INTRODUCTION

Democracy is a form of government in which the people hold all or most of the political power. In democracies, government officials are expected to take actions and implement policies that reflect the will of the majority of the citizenry. In other political systems, the rulers generally rule for their own benefit, or at least they usually put their own interests first. This results in deep differences between the rulers and the average citizen. In undemocratic states, elites enjoy far more privileges and advantages than the average citizen. Indeed, autocratic governments are often created to exploit the average citizen.

Elections allow citizens to choose representatives to make choices for them, and under some circumstances to decide major issues themselves. Yet democracy is much more than campaigns and elections. Many nations conduct elections but are not democratic. True democracy is dependent on a range of freedoms for its citizenry, and it simultaneously exists to protect and enhance those freedoms. At its best, democracy ensures that elites, average citizens, and even groups on the margins of society all have the same rights, privileges, and opportunities. The components of democracy have changed over time as individuals and groups have struggled to expand equality. In doing so, the very notion of what makes up a democracy has evolved. The volumes in this series examine the core freedoms that form the foundation of modern democracy.

Citizenship and Immigration explores what it means to be a citizen in a democracy. The principles of democracy are based on equality, liberty, and government by the consent of the people. Equality means that all citizens have the same rights and responsibilities. Democracies have struggled to integrate all groups and ensure full equality. Citizenship in a democracy is the formal recognition that a person is a member of the country's political community. Modern democracies have faced profound debates over immigration, especially how many people to admit to the country and what rights to confer on immigrants who are not citizens.

Challenges have also emerged within democracies over how to ensure disadvantaged groups enjoy full equality with the majority, or traditionally dominant, populations. While outdated legal or political barriers have been mostly removed, democracies still struggle to overcome cultural or economic impediments to equality. *Gender Equality and Identity Rights*

7

analyzes why gender equality has proven especially challenging, requiring political, economic, and cultural reforms. Concurrently, *Religious, Cultural, and Minority Rights* surveys the efforts that democracies have undertaken to integrate disadvantaged groups into the political, economic, and social mainstream.

A free and unfettered media provides an important check on government power and ensures an informed citizenry. The importance of free expression and a free press are detailed in *Speech, Media, and Protest*, while *Employment and Workers' Rights* provides readers with an overview of the importance of economic liberty and the ways in which employment and workers' rights reinforce equality by guaranteeing opportunity.

The maintenance of both liberty and equality requires a legal system in which the police are constrained by the rule of law. This means that security officials understand and respect the rights of individuals and groups and use their power in a manner that benefits communities, not represses them. While this is the ideal, legal systems continue to struggle to achieve equality, especially among disadvantaged groups. These topics form the core of *Justice, Policing, and the Rule of Law.*

Corruption and Transparency examines the greatest danger to democracy: corruption. Corruption can undermine people's faith in government and erode equality. Transparency, or open government, provides the best means to prevent corruption by ensuring that the decisions and actions of officials are easily understood.

As discussed in *Political Participation and Voting Rights*, a government of the people requires its citizens to provide regular input on policies and decisions through consultations and voting. Despite the importance of voting, the history of democracies has been marked by the struggle to expand voting rights. Many groups, including women, only gained the right to vote in the last century, and continue to be underrepresented in political office.

Ultimately, all of the foundations of democracy are interrelated. Equality ensures liberty, while liberty helps maintain equality. Meanwhile, both are necessary for a government by consent to be effective and lasting. Within a democracy, all people must be treated equally and be able to enjoy the full range of liberties of the country, including rights such as free speech, religion, and voting.

—Tom Lansford

CHAPTER ONE

RELIGION

WORDS TO UNDERSTAND

belief: an acceptance of a statement or idea concerning a religion or faith.

doctrine: defines the principle beliefs of a religion, both spoken and written.

dogma: a set of principles established by an authority as true.

faith: a set of unchangeable conditions concerning a higher power, based on spiritual apprehension rather than proof.

mythos: a set of stories or texts that describe and reinforce the beliefs of a religion.

ritual: a set of activities or actions that are designed to show that a person is a member of the group and believes the same things as the other members.

sect: a group of like-minded people who share the same ideas.

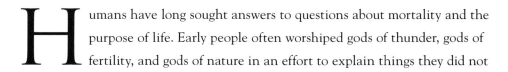

H umans have long sought answers to questions about mortality and the purpose of life. Early people often worshiped gods of thunder, gods of fertility, and gods of nature in an effort to explain things they did not understand. Humans have turned to religion for millennia in an attempt to answer these questions, but some religions state that questions about nature are answered through divine inspiration, and that a higher power has given them the answers. Some people, meanwhile, have decided that the right choice for them is not to follow any religion. An atheist is someone who does not believe there is a god, while an agnostic is someone who feels humans can never be certain if there is a god or not. Nonetheless, there are many religious and nonreligious people on the Earth, so how do we attempt to understand the variety of religion without trying to say which one is right or wrong? How does something so varied and private play into government systems and rights? We will discuss these issues in the coming chapters.

How Do We Describe Religion?

How do we attempt to describe and understand a religion if we are not part of it? We start with the terms used to describe all religions. Let us start with the idea of faith, which is a set of conditions concerning a higher power that are based on spiritual apprehension rather than proof. For example, Christianity, Islam, Hinduism, Buddhism, and Judaism are all faiths. We describe these religions as the Christian faith, the Islamic faith, and so forth. The important thing about a faith is that it defines the religion; it cannot change or the religion changes.

The second term to understand is belief. A belief is an acceptance of a statement or idea concerning the faith that can change over time, as long as it does not undermine the faith itself. For example, in the Christian faith, there are varying beliefs that have led to denominations other than the Roman Catholic Church. Martin Luther was the catalyst for the Protestant Reformation when he posted his 95 theses to the door of the All Saints' Catholic Church in Wittenberg, Germany, on October 31, 1517. Most non-Catholics are called "Protestants," based on their individual protests against certain Catholic teachings. Lutherans, Baptists, Methodists, and the like are all Protestants, but they are still part of the Christian faith.

Young Buddhist monks in Thailand.

Belief is usually illustrated through **mythos**, a set of stories or texts that describe and reinforce the belief of the faith. Mythos is not to be confused with mythology, which is the study of stories about god and gods, specifically Greek and Roman mythology. The collected mythos of a religion supports the religion's **dogma**. **Doctrine** specifically defines the principle beliefs of the religion, both spoken and written. The whole set of beliefs, mythos, dogma, and doctrine helps to define the **sect**. For instance,

RELIGIOUS BUILDINGS

Religious buildings can be a good indicator of what religion is (or was) popular in a particular area. These buildings have many different names, depending on the religion itself. Christianity calls its buildings churches, Islam calls its buildings mosques, Hinduism and Buddhism call their buildings temples, and Judaism calls its buildings synagogues. Some religions want to be seen through their architecture. Think about the tall steeples on Christian churches or prayer towers on mosques. These buildings become icons for the presence of the religion. In some areas the buildings may have been converted from a mosque to a church, or vice versa, but you can sometimes tell what the original use was based on its architecture.

A mosque in Istanbul, Turkey.

Islam and Christianity have many different sects, but each of them is still part of the main religious grouping.

One way that a religion can show that members belong to a sect is by performing **rituals**. An example of ritual is attendance at a church, mosque, temple, or synagogue on certain days or times for worship. Rituals are typically the most visible part of a religion to people who do not follow the religion.

What Types of Religion Exist?

Various types of religions exist throughout the world. We can describe most religions as being either inclusive or exclusive, and as either universalizing or ethnic. An *inclusive religion* is a religion that believes there are multiple paths to understanding the higher power or achieving the goals of any religion. Examples of inclusive religions are Hinduism and Buddhism.

Conversely, an *exclusive religion* asserts that followers are the only people who understand the pathway to God or the higher power, and that one must follow that guide if they are to be part of the religion. Islam and Christianity are good examples of exclusive religions. However, Islam and Christianity are not just exclusive religions; they are also universalizing. A *universalizing religion* is a one that allows for anyone to convert to the faith, and in fact members are morally required to attempt to convert people to their religion. Missionary activity is very common in universalizing religions, which helps the religion spread by conversions to the faith.

Faiths that one must be born into are known as *ethnic religions*. Missionary activities are not necessary, because everyone knows who belongs based on their heritage. Examples of ethnic religions are Judaism and Hinduism; children of Hindu or Jewish parents are automatically part of the religion by a blood relationship. It is possible, however, for people of other ethnicities to convert to, or at least participate in, an ethnic religion. Ethnic religions typically grow as quickly as the population, while universalizing religions grow as quickly as conversions occur.

A traditional orthodox Jewish man prays by the Western (or "Wailing") Wall in Jerusalem.

HOW DO RELIGIONS EXPRESS THEMSELVES IN SOCIETIES?

In society, religions can play an interesting role. Religion has the potential to provide a moral and ethical compass and even help unify a country, but it can also be problematic if there are many religions or there is no religious tolerance between the religions and nonreligious people. In Poland, over 88 percent of the population is Roman Catholic, so there tends to be cultural harmony among religious people. In Northern Ireland, however, Catholics and Protestants have fought over religious and political differences for hundreds of years. In Afghanistan, areas controlled by the Taliban do not allow any religion except Sunni Islam, and all other religious viewpoints are violently eliminated. Since religion

---

 ### ORTHODOX VERSUS HETERODOX

Many religions have a classification called *orthodox*, which means a strict interpretation of their religion's traditional laws as prescribed by a religious authority. In English, the opposite of orthodox is unorthodox, but with religions we use the term *heterodox*, meaning different beliefs. Typically, in most religions there are orthodox views and heterodox views. The Catholic Church and Eastern Orthodox Church are good examples of orthodox beliefs in Christianity, while most of the Protestant Churches (i.e., Lutherans, Baptists, and Methodists) are heterodox. In Islam, any belief that enforces strict interpretations of the Quran, the holy text of Islam, and the hadith, the teachings of Muhammad, is orthodox, while the beliefs that relax the literal interpretation are heterodox. The argument among religious people for orthodox behavior is that the religion has rules that have to be followed, while the argument for heterodox behavior is that the religion has to be understood in its historical and cultural context, and the rules that were necessary hundreds of years ago may not be applicable to today's society.

---

and one's beliefs tend to be private, religion usually plays a bigger role in a society if there are visual clues to religious behavior or the religion is very active in the country. Think about religion in your country. How do you know what religions are present? Are there many, or just a few?

Architecture can be an easy indicator if there are religious buildings like churches, prayer towers, and temples. However, does a religious group have the right to erect a building wherever it wants to? What if the group is in the minority or wants to build next to a religion that does not want them there? Some religions do not build formal or uniquely identifiable structures. So how would you know they existed? Questions about religious freedom are difficult if the religion in question is a minority within a democracy.

Young Sikhs in their traditional turbans.

RELIGIOUS RITUALS

Rituals exist in most cultures, often without any religious meaning. A birthday party with gifts, cake, and candles is part of the ritual of celebrating growing a year older. Most all religions have rituals that highlight and express the religious experience. When members of a group all do the same thing together, it shows an outward sign of unity. Christian rituals include attending church on a certain day, praying, singing songs, and baptisms. Islamic rituals included praying five times a day as a group, attending mosque on certain days, and making a pilgrimage to Mecca. Religious rituals are visual indicators that one belongs to a certain group.

Thousands of pilgrims at the al-Haram Mosque in Mecca in 2008. It is considered a religious duty of Muslims to make this pilgrimage (hajj) at some point in their lives.

Religions can be visible if there are rituals performed by the group, such as styles of clothing, gathering in open spaces, or attending religious services in buildings on certain days. The Sikhs are known for wearing turbans with a "rishi" knot in the front; commonly it is orange to represent courage and wisdom, but it can be blue, white, or black. Certain groups of Pentecostal women wear plain long skirts and long hair. Costumes and outfits are easy outside identifiers of religious conformity.

Some religions are very private, and it may be difficult to tell if they are even present. However, ritual and religious practice can be evident through prayer, meditation, or even a moment of silence before events as small as dinner or as large as a sporting event. In a democracy, there is a delicate balance between allowing true freedom of religion and allowing the majority religion or majority nonreligious to dictate the rules for all other religions in a way that limits religious freedom.

TEXT-DEPENDENT QUESTIONS

1. What are ways that a religion can be identified by visual clues only?
2. What is the difference between an inclusive and exclusive religion?
3. What are rituals that are performed by a religious group in your country?

RESEARCH PROJECTS

1. List the religious buildings in your neighborhood or city and compare them to see what religion is most apparent. Create a chart grouping each building by religious faith.
2. Do a search on religious buildings and see if you can identify symbols and styles that are unique to each religion. Sketch the dominant symbols that are part of various religious buildings.

CHAPTER TWO

RELIGIOUS RIGHTS

 ## WORDS TO UNDERSTAND

religious conviction: when a group of people remain steadfast in their personal beliefs even in light of great pressure to change their stance or adopt an opposing viewpoint.

religious persecution: when members of a religious group are punished or even killed solely for their beliefs.

religious tolerance: when one religion allows another to exist alongside it, without interference.

secular state: governments that are not officially influenced by religion in making decisions.

theocracy: a system of government in which all major decisions are made under the guidance of religious leaders' interpretation of divine authority.

Some parts of the world continue to operate with a combination of religion and government, where all major decisions are made under the guidance of religious leaders' interpretation of divine authority. These governments are called **theocracies**. They are often seen as being fundamentally different from democracies, where the population makes collective decisions. In theocracies, the

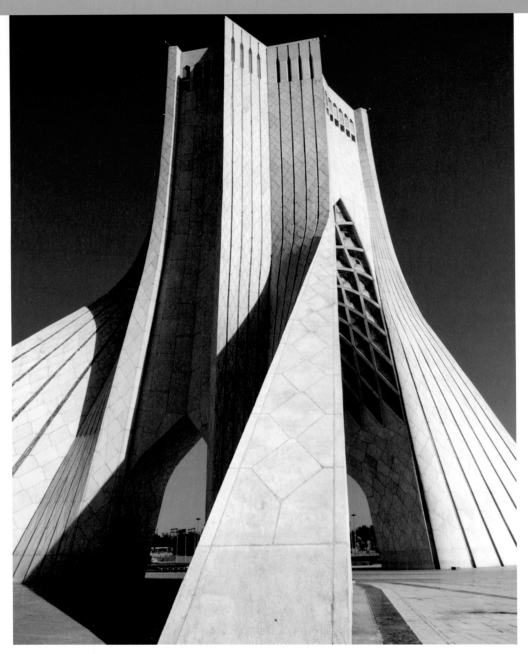

Theocracies are not as common in modern times as they once were; the government of Iran is one of the few still considered to be theocratic. The Azadi ("Freedom") Tower was built in 1971 to celebrate 2,500th anniversary of the Persian empire.

leader of the country and the leader of the religion are often the same person. Theocracies do not require majority rule, and they can even limit the religious freedom of minority religions. However, there are many countries that have a majority that are religious, but that have chosen to have a government system that includes a separation of church and state.

Governments that are not officially influenced by religion in governing decisions are called **secular states**. *Secular* is a term that is applied to behaviors or governments that have no religious or spiritual basis. A secular state is one that is officially neutral to all religions in its territory. Almost every democracy has to function as a secular state to avoid the dominant religion from turning the country into a theocracy or restricting the religious and civic freedom of minorities.

FREEDOM OF RELIGION IN SECULAR STATES

Article 9 of the European Convention on Human Rights, signed by all 47 members of the Council of Europe states, "Everyone has the right to freedom of thought, conscience, and religion; this right includes freedom to change his religion or belief and freedom, either alone or in community with others and in public or private, to manifest his religion or belief, in worship, teaching, practice, and observance." The U.S. Constitution protects the freedom of religion in the First Amendment of the Bill of Rights. Specifically, it states, "Congress shall make no law respecting an establishment of religion, or prohibiting the free exercise thereof." The U.S. Supreme Court, in the 1943 case *West Virginia State Board of Education v. Barnette*, ruled that that no government official, high or petty, can make anyone salute the flag, pray, declare their religion, or tell their political opinion.

The idea that religion can be freely practiced is common in democratic nations, but that practice cannot impede someone else from practicing their religion. The Universal Declaration of Human Rights, adopted by the United Nations (UN) in 1948, is very specific regarding the importance of every person having the right to determine his or her faith and creed according to conscience. Even though the declaration is not a legally

AMISH RELIGIOUS RIGHTS

The Amish community started in Switzerland in 1693 when Jakob Ammann split from the Anabaptists. The people who agreed with Ammann became the Amish people. The Amish immigrated to Pennsylvania in the United States for various reasons in the early 1900s, and then spread to Ohio and Indiana. For religious reasons, the Amish try to avoid using all forms of modern technology, from electricity to automobiles, because they believe it to be a distraction from the way humans should live. The Amish follow a set of guidelines called the Ordnung, a German word meaning order, disciple, arrangement, organization, or system. Because the Amish avoid many modern technologies, they tend to stand out with their horse-drawn carriages and style of dress. The Amish have a religious right to exist with their culture and worship their God the way they see fit. Many cities and communities around the Amish settlements make sure that they do not interfere with the Amish way of life and allow them to peacefully exist.

An Amish buggy in traffic.

binding document, the UN recognizes that all people should have the right to express their religious beliefs in worship, teaching, and practice, and to proclaim those beliefs in a social setting. Further, the declaration states that every person has the right to associate with others for religious purposes. The overarching idea is that all people can choose their religion and that they should have the right to peacefully practice their religion without fear of losing that right to a government vote.

COUNTRIES WITH A DOMINANT RELIGION

In a democracy where the dominant religion is in the majority, one would think there should be no issues with religious rights. But since most democratic countries are also secular states, it is usually necessary to ensure the right to practice the majority religion for that religion to give up the power to a secular state.

Democracy can become one-sided when there is a majority religion and members of that religion vote to allow only their religion the right and freedom to practice. The temptation for the majority to vote out other religions or religious beliefs can be strong, and a concerted effort may be needed to prevent such actions. Slovakia has not allowed for any mosques to be built in the country, and it remains the only European Union country without a mosque. However, the absence of a mosque in Slovakia restricts the ability of Muslims to practice their faith in that country. The concept of one religion allowing another to exist alongside of it, without interference, is called **religious tolerance**. Democracy and majority rule requires the majority to not dictate everything to the minority, including religious viewpoints.

COUNTRIES WITH MINORITY RELIGIONS

Every country has minority religions if more than one religion exists. Sometimes a religious group is very small compared to the other religion or religions in the country. How can members of such a religion be guaranteed the right to practice their religion? Why would these individuals choose to not follow the majority religion?

HEAD COVERING

Many religions, Christianity and Islam included, practice the religious tradition of head covering. Head covering can be achieved with a simple scarf, or it can be more elaborate with very ornate designs. Many religions use head coverings as a sign of respect and reverence to their god or gods. One extreme example is the full-body burqa, which covers the entire body. However, nuns, clergy, rabbis, imams, and gurus all wear some type of head covering for religious reasons. This practice brings up the question of whether a secular state can require that head coverings not be used in public.

In 2010, France made head covering illegal if it covers the face, because it was determined that seeing individual faces was important for national security. France banned all forms of face coverings, from masks to helmets to burqas. Some argued, however, that this violated an individual's religious right to practice head covering. The French government disagreed, saying that *any* women who do not allow themselves to be identified are unable to pass through a security check. If the law specifically listed only religious types of face coverings, it would likely be a violation of religious rights. Instead, the law requires that all people be identifiable.

A Muslim mother and daughter in traditional head coverings.

The term **religious conviction** describes a group of people who are steadfast in their personal beliefs, even in light of great pressure to change their stance or to adopt an opposing viewpoint. When members of a group are punished or even killed solely for their beliefs, we call this **religious persecution**. In parts of Syria and the Sudan, people are routinely thrown in jail for not being the "right" religion. In a democracy, being in the minority should not mean that you cannot practice your religion.

What happens when a law is passed that is against the religious convictions of a minority religion? Some Native Americans in the United States use bald eagle feathers in their religious ceremonies. However, the bald eagle is a federally protected species, which means that it is illegal to even possess eagle feathers. The federal government tried to stop the practice, but they lost in court on the grounds of religious freedom. Native Americans cannot kill or capture eagles for their feathers, but they can now seek a permit to possess the feathers if their tribe is federally recognized.

When do religious rights trump the democratically elected law of the land? Sikhs carry a religiously important knife called the *kirpan*, which must be carried at all times. Can they bring these into government buildings or onto airplanes?

A Cree headdress made with eagle feathers, from around 1940.

In India, Sikhs can bring a *kirpan* onto a plane, but in Europe they cannot. How can we know if or when religious rights are being violated?

RELIGIOUS RIGHTS VIOLATIONS

Most democracies are secular states, and in a democracy, there are laws that protect citizens' freedom to practice their religions. Freedom of religion is applied to all religions, as long as they do not break the laws of the land. Creating laws in a democracy requires that religious freedom and liberties are still respected on both organizational and personal levels. If a law is passed that places a restriction on a religious holiday, it is a violation of that religion's rights. The government cannot sponsor or promote a religious holiday, nor can it prevent a religious holiday from being privately observed. Nations must allow for a religion to gather in and maintain buildings for religious services. The state must allow religions to follow their religious laws, dress according to their customs, and access their

 RELIGIOUS FOOD TABOOS

Many religions have restrictions on the types of food that members can and cannot eat. In 1996, McDonald's opened its first restaurant in India. In 2001 the chain faced a $100 million lawsuit for selling Hindus "vegetarian fries" that were flavored with beef fat, even though McDonald's had claimed that the fries did not contain any beef or animal by-products. The Hindu religion restricts eating any beef, and McDonald's changed their recipe and apologized.

Food restrictions are not uncommon in religions. Judaism and Seventh Day Adventists do not eat pork or shellfish, Muslims do not eat pork, and Catholics do not eat meat on certain days. To respect individual's religious rights, it needs to be communicated if anything is being served that is in violation of their religious laws and customs.

The First Church of Christ, Scientist in Boston. This is the Mother Church of the Christian Science faith.

religious buildings, or it is violating religious rights. A secular state cannot pass laws that punish people for not following the majority religion, like punishments for blasphemy, forcing conversions, or forced observances of religious rituals or holidays.

For a democracy to pass a law that conflicts with a religious belief, it must pass a "rational basis test." The law must be directly related to government interests, like helping people avoid harm, improving civil opportunity, or maintaining the rights of others, in order to pass the rational basis test. For example, many countries require vaccination of newborns to reduce the spread of disease. However, followers of a religion called Christian Science do not believe that babies should be given any medicine, including vaccinations. Thus, Christian Scientists might claim that mandatory vaccinations violate their religious freedom. But in a secular state, they are not allowed to make this claim, because the right to health is a right of all humans. Christian Science does not require its followers to avoid all medical care if state laws require them. In this case, Christian Science made concessions to the state when it comes to child care. However, it is the prerogative of *adult* Christian Scientists to refuse medical care based on religious reasons. Each democracy protects the rights of religion, within reason. Just because a religion declares its rules, those rules do not automatically become protected under the tenets of religious freedom.

TEXT-DEPENDENT QUESTIONS

1. What are examples of violations of religious rights?
2. What international laws exist that protect the freedom of religion?
3. How can a religious law be against state law without violating religious rights?

RESEARCH PROJECTS

1. Do an Internet search on religious freedom violations in your country. Read over the issues and choose one to discuss. What is your opinion on the topic? Should religious rights be upheld, or should secular law be upheld? Explain your reasoning.
2. Create a list of the religions in your country. What laws are present in your country to protect both majority and minority religions?

CHAPTER THREE

HUMAN CULTURE

 WORDS TO UNDERSTAND

cultural area: the spatial component to a group of people.

cultural ecology: how well a group of people incorporates or changes their environmental surroundings.

cultural hearth: where an idea and innovation originates.

cultural history: the common events a group has experienced over time.

cultural landscape: how a group manifests itself on the Earth, and how its members have reshaped the land where they live.

folk culture: a unifying physical expression of everyday life by a local group of people.

The term *culture* originates from the Latin word *cultus*, which roughly translates as "to care for." We derive the term *cultivate* from the same Latin phrase to describe how we take care of and grow plants. Similarly, humans develop their cultures by fostering the things they care for and eliminating the things they do not like. In this sense, culture is the manifestation of human collective intellect. People tend to rank their standards of behavior by importance, and we call these standards *values*. Culture develops as an exchange of ideas and values over time.

Children taking part in an annual folk-dancing festival in Greece, 2014.

Cultural groups have decided on appropriate behaviors and morals over time. For example, we know that if everyone lies all the time, we cannot trust anyone, so lying is held as a negative behavior in our values as a society. Humans learn many aspects of their culture as they grow up. Human beings do not possess too many inherent abilities at birth, so they learn behavior from the culture in which they are raised. Each cultural group teaches their offspring the acceptable behaviors and values of the group to the benefit of the society. People tend to adopt the language, religion, values, and culture of their cultural group. People are social beings, meaning that they typically exist in groups, and they have to learn what behavior is acceptable within their group. Because people exist all around the Earth, they can grow up in distinctively different areas and develop different ideas and values. As people grow and experience other cultures, they can change or incorporate the values and behaviors of other cultures.

We can trace many cultural values and behaviors back to a point of origin. Where an idea or innovation starts is called a **cultural hearth**, invoking the idea that people once gathered around a fire and exchanged ideas. Human culture developed over many years to be what we see today, but all ideas start somewhere. These ideas get spread around the world through various types of cultural diffusion when different groups exchange ideas. Modern behaviors developed over many centuries, but every idea and innovation started somewhere.

Cultures develop ideas, behavior, and skills over time. Most cultures developed as **folk culture**, which is a unifying physical expression of everyday life by a local group of people. Folk culture is often evident through the distinctive traditions, types of clothing, and music of a small group of people. When many cultures developed, they did not move around much over a long period of time, so folk cultures can be very distinctive, even compared to neighboring groups. These local communities developed their ideas, behaviors, and skills separately from others. Folk culture manifests itself as different styles of dress, different dialects, different accents, and different cultural rituals. Estonia is a great example of a folk culture where playing the zither and wearing folk clothing is a long-standing tradition. The annual four-day folk culture celebration

The Europeade 2011 was held in Tartu, Estonia.

called the Europeade is a showcase of unique European cultures, with over 250 regions being represented in 2015. All of the cultures that participated developed over a long period of time.

Many modern countries have developed a new type of culture known as "popular culture." Often shortened to "pop" culture, it is shared behavior or expression of desire across large masses of people, not just local groups. Pop culture requires mass production and mass marketing to allow for a unified product to be delivered. The Internet and television have allowed for ideas and products to be spread throughout

 ## DIA DE LOS MUERTOS

In much of Latin America, especially Mexico, a tradition to honor the deceased is celebrated on November 1, All Souls Day, called Dia de los Muertos (Day of the Dead). This traditional holiday is celebrated by many around the world as their cultural right. The reason the dead are celebrated is because the culture believes that the deceased would be insulted by mourning or sadness, and therefore these cultures prefer celebrating the lives of their ancestors. The day is marked by bright costumes, food, drink, parties, and any activities the dead enjoyed while alive. *Calacas* (skeletons) and *claveras* (skulls) are found everywhere during the holiday, showing the recognition of death as part of life and the remembrance of one's ancestors. People even dress up as skeletons, but they are always in fancy clothes, as if attending a party. To people outside the culture, this celebration can seem strange, but once one learns about the meaning of the holiday, it makes a lot more sense.

Papier-mâché Day of the Dead figures from Guanajuato Market, in Mexico.

MARDI GRAS

A cultural holiday with deep roots in religion is Mardi Gras, or Fat Tuesday, marking the beginning of Lent on Ash Wednesday. However, even though most Catholics celebrate Mardi Gras, it has become a huge cultural celebration, even for the nonreligious. Mardi Gras is celebrated with parades, costuming, and events throughout the day. In Brazil, Carnival (what Mardi Gras is called there) is their most famous holiday. Mardi Gras is celebrated in many places in the United States, in the cities like New Orleans, Mobile, and Galveston, as well as in the countries of Italy, France, and Germany. Many of the Mardi Gras celebrations start months before the actual day as part of a cultural history and social bond.

The Krewe of Rex parade through New Orleans on Mardi Gras.

societies. Most modern marketing is about selling mass-produced brand-name products. Pop culture is expressed in all kinds of ways, including types of music, clothing, food, and even electronic products like cell phones. In a way, where folk culture helped to make groups of people very different, globalized pop culture is unifying people through shared artifacts and culture.

CULTURAL EXPRESSION

The term *cultural expression* refers to how a group of people can be identified. It is divided up into *cultural history*, *cultural landscape*, *cultural area*, and *cultural ecology*. **Cultural history** refers to all of the experiences shared over time by a particular group. If members of a group suffered a famine or migrated to the same region at the same time, their shared events can be a cultural unifier through a shared cultural history. Often, very old cultural groups prefer to keep their traditional methods and values, rather than accepting new ones. They may prefer folk culture over pop culture, or make great efforts to be sure traditional practices are continued.

Cultural landscape refers to how a group of people changes the physical topography where they live. Think about the buildings, roads, electrical lines, dams, canals, and so on that make up your surroundings. How many of these are human constructs, and how many would be there without human interaction? Try to think of the cultural landscape of what would remain behind if all humans were instantly removed. What could we learn from the landscape without even asking anyone? Could we identify a particular group of people as different from their neighbors just based on the landscape changes they carried out? How far would we need to go before the cultural landscape looked significantly different?

Cultural area refers to the spatial component of a group of people. How much space do they take up? How large a space do they have influence over? How far do you have to go to get to another cultural area? Some cultural areas can be very large, while others are very small. If we tried to identify the cultural area of democracy

A man in traditional Aboriginal dress and body paint near Queensland, Australia.

SAINT PATRICK'S DAY

Celebrated on March 17, Saint Patrick's Day is a cultural celebration honoring Saint Patrick, the patron saint of Ireland, and Irish culture in general. In Ireland this holiday is mainly a religious feast day, but around the world, especially where Irish immigrants have settled, the holiday is more of a cultural celebration. The first Saint Patrick's Day was held in the United States in 1737 in Boston.

Parades are held in honor of Irish culture, and green becomes a dominant color in cities around the world, including London, Barcelona, Copenhagen, Boston, New York, Chicago, and New Orleans. In Chicago, the city even dyes the Chicago River green for the day. The Irish proudly share their culture, even—perhaps especially—those who no longer live in Ireland.

Crowds awaiting the annual St. Patrick's Day Parade in New York City.

as governance, the area covered would be global, with only a few exceptions. If we tried to identify the cultural area of *pagne* clothing, a brightly colored wrap, the area covered will be predominantly western Africa. Each cultural trait will have a different cultural area.

Finally, we can look at a group of people and see how well they get along with their natural surroundings. This is called **cultural ecology**. Does this group completely change nature or live alongside it? Often, cultural landscape helps to identify if the cultural group incorporates nature or changes it. Some cultures completely rely upon nature and try to preserve nature, like the Aborigines of Australia or the Inuit of North America, while other cultures only preserve parks or gardens. When we look at all the different forms of cultural expression all together, we can begin to understand that culture a bit better.

TEXT-DEPENDENT QUESTIONS

1. What is the difference between folk culture and popular culture?
2. Why places of innovation are called cultural hearths?
3. What are some different types of cultural expression?

RESEARCH PROJECTS

1. Examine your day-to-day life and make a list of how cultural landscape has manifested itself.
2. List things that exist in your daily life, such as food, clothing, electronics, and transportation. From a popular cultural standpoint, how many of these things are available in many other parts of the world?

CHAPTER FOUR

CULTURAL AND HUMAN RIGHTS

WORDS TO UNDERSTAND

centrifugal force: a force that pulls people apart or causes a country to break up.

centripetal force: a force that brings people and societies together.

cultural identity: those things that collectively help people feel they belong to a group.

cultural persecution: when cultural rights are not allowed or are actively oppressed.

melting pot: a wide range of cultural differences, all in a small area, that get along with each other.

refugees: people who are kicked out of their country or forced to flee to another country because they are not welcome or fear for their lives.

A right is a moral or legal entitlement to act or behave in a certain way. Human and cultural rights are defined by Article 27 of the Universal Declaration of Human Rights, adopted by the United Nations in 1948. The declaration states that everyone has the right to freely participate in the cultural life of the community, to enjoy the arts, and to share in scientific advancement and its benefits.

The United Nations Educational, Scientific and Cultural Organization (UNESCO) wrote in its Principles of International Cultural Co-operation that each culture has a dignity and value that must be respected and preserved, and that every culture has the right and the duty to develop. World organizations clearly emphasize the importance of diversity and the value of cultural development. All humans should be granted certain rights.

Cultural Rights

Cultural rights are human rights for a group of people as related to behavior and arts. Article 17 of the charter of the African Commission on Human and People's Rights guarantees that individuals have a right to participate in the cultural life of their community. Article 13 of the American Declaration of the Rights and Duties of Man, adopted by the Ninth International Conference of American States in 1948, states the same thing: all people have the right to participate in the cultural life of their community. Most regions on Earth have a human rights declaration that articulates the right to participate in a group's culture.

Humans who feel they belong to a group can have what is called a **cultural identity**. A cultural identity can be very important to an individual, even if one does not or cannot practice that culture. Oftentimes, people who move away from their home or home country bring their own cultural identity with them. When groups of people with similar cultural identities move to the same area, they can re-create parts or all of their culture. Little India in Singapore, Chinatown in Toronto, Canada, and Little Italy in New York are examples of ethnic neighborhoods where people retain their cultural identity even outside their country of origin. Cultural identity can manifest as types of food and styles of dress, dance, art, and music. Cultural rights ultimately mean that a group of people can enjoy their own culture and its components with equality, dignity,

A statue of Ganesha at Sri Veeramakaliamman Temple in Little India, Singapore.

and nondiscrimination by others. People have the right to their culture and should be allowed to live their culture.

CENTRIPETAL AND CENTRIFUGAL FORCES

Many times, the issue of cultural rights arises when there is something that divides two groups of people. We call forces that bring people and societies together **centripetal forces**. The forces that pull people apart are called **centrifugal forces**. These two forces either bring people together or push them apart.

Language is a great example of how a single thing can be either a cultural barrier or a cultural unifier. If two groups cannot communicate, they tend to not mingle, so it is considered a centrifugal force. However, a common language can be a reason people stay together, so it can be considered a centripetal force. Other examples of things that bring people together or pull them apart are political affiliations, religion, cultural history, gender, race, and ethnicity. As long as centripetal forces, or reasons

 CZECHOSLOVAKIA

In 1918, Czechoslovakia declared itself independent of the Austro-Hungarian Empire. From 1948 to 1990, Czechoslovakia was part of the Eastern Bloc of Soviet-controlled Europe. But the people of Czechoslovakia slowly decided that they would be better as two countries instead of just one. The Czechs and Slovaks speak different languages and have different cultural histories and separate media systems. From 1948 to 1990, the powerful Soviet state acted as a centripetal force keeping the Czechs and Slovaks together. Once Soviet authority was gone and democracy returned, however, the centrifugal forces were stronger than the centripetal forces. Czechoslovakia peacefully divided to form the Czech Republic and Slovakia in 1993.

Syrian refugees at a camp near Atmeh, on the Turkish border, in January 2013.

to stay together, are stronger than centrifugal forces, or reasons to break apart, the society remains together.

Cultural Manifestation

Cultures can manifest themselves in both overt and covert manners. Overt culture is easy to identify because it is apparent when you see it. The way people dress, how people act, the things people use—these are all types of visual culture. Do you eat food with a fork, like they do in Europe and the United States; with chopsticks, like they do in East Asia; or with your hands, like they do in southern India? Do you carry a smartphone, a computer, or nothing at all? Overt culture is a simple way that humans categorize people.

Covert culture is usually still evident, but many people do it without even thinking about it. Covert culture is culture that is overlooked or not readily noticed. Food is a great example of covert culture. What food do you eat, and what would you not eat? What

BASQUE LANGUAGE RIGHTS

The Basque region in Spain and France is a unique cultural area. The Basque culture existed before the Roman Empire, and its language, Euskara, is not related to any other European language, meaning we cannot trace its origin. In Spain, General Francisco Franco rose to power during the Spanish Civil War (1936–1939) and formed a fascist government that lasted until 1975. During that time, Franco made it illegal to speak Euskara, and illegal for schools to teach it. Those who spoke it would be thrown into jail. In spite of great effort to get rid of the Basque language and culture, however, they persisted. In the late 1960s, the Euskaltzaindia (Academy of Basque Language) developed a standardization of the language to help bridge dialect differences. The new unified Basque language became known as Euskara Batua. By 1976 the Basque government was using the new unified Batua language. Spain now has laws in place protecting the use of Euskara.

A banner supporting the pro-Basque forces from 2011.

style of food do you like? What does your house look like? How is your house furnished? Music choice can also be a cultural indicator. Do you like Celtic music, blues, Eurobeat, rock, classical, or something else? Culturally, as a group, you are deciding what music, food, and behavior you like. Certain traditions can define different cultural groups, like what holidays are celebrated or what traditions are followed. When there is a wide range of cultural differences in a small area that all exists peacefully, we call this a **melting pot**, invoking the idea of throwing different things into a pot, which all melt together to make one stew. In countries with many cultures without a clear majority, or where many cultures exist in peace, these are called multicultural countries. Examples include Belgium, Canada, and the Netherlands.

CULTURAL RIGHTS VIOLATIONS

In some countries cultural rights are not allowed or are actively oppressed. This is known as **cultural persecution**. Examples of persecution can be as simple as not allowing a public display of a holiday item, like not allowing Christmas displays, or as extreme as genocide, the attempt to kill everyone in a particular group, such as the Bosnian Muslims in the former Yugoslavia. Typically, cultural rights are violated by not letting one group speak their own language, or gather for cultural events, but other types of cultural rights violations exist, too.

Sometimes a group decides to force another group from their neighborhood or city just because they have a different culture. In this case, the group that is forced to move is having their cultural rights violated, because all humans have the right to their own culture and cultural expression. People who are ejected from their country or are forced to flee to another country because they believe themselves to be unsafe there are called **refugees**. For example, millions of Syrians left their home country in 2015 because of the extreme levels of violence. The basic human rights of everyone include the right to adequate housing, the right to health, the right to dignity, the right to work, and the right to have access to food, water, and sanitation.

Signs welcoming Syrian refugees at a demonstration in Scotland in 2015.

Discrimination is the practice of distinguishing between cultural groups based on class, race, gender, religion, or political opinions. Discrimination can be positive or negative. If people are chosen for work more often because they are more similar to the majority culture, the employers are discriminating by choosing the majority group. Often, however, discrimination leads to cultural and human rights violations. Worse, if discrimination lasts for a very long time, it can lead to false impressions and stereotypes of cultures and gender roles, such as the idea that women are not good at math, or that farmers are not intelligent. These ideas are erroneous.

Many democracies attempt to protect against cultural rights violations by passing laws of inclusion and diversity. For example, freedom of speech and the freedom to assemble are often used to protect minority cultural rights. The challenge to democracy is to view society as making laws that are best for "we," rather than best for "me." Minority cultures should still be allowed to exist because they add diversity and value to a society. Cultural rights are naturally protected in a democracy by allowing for free and genuine elections through universal suffrage, along with freedom of information, as long as the majority does not abuse its authority.

TEXT-DEPENDENT QUESTIONS

1. What is the consistent theme among the various human rights declarations?
2. What are examples of hidden and visual culture?
3. How can one's cultural rights be violated?

RESEARCH PROJECTS

1. Go to the website of the United Nations Refugee Agency (www.unhcr.org) and find out the origin of the latest wave of refugees. Research the reasons why they are leaving, and write an essay explaining these reasons.
2. Think about centripetal and centrifugal forces. What are things that bring your community together, and what are things that keep them apart? Use examples of language, religion, political views, and cultural background in a chart that highlights the differences.

CHAPTER FIVE

MINORITY RIGHTS

 ## WORDS TO UNDERSTAND

ethnic cleansing: a policy of getting rid of an entire group of people because they are unwanted or different.

ethnic conflict: when differences of ethnicity and culture develop to the point that one or both of the groups involved are willing to fight.

ethnicity: a state of belonging to a cultural group with a common history or cultural system.

minority: a cultural group that is outnumbered by another cultural group.

race: an identification based solely on visual identifiers such as skin color or facial features.

racism: the idea that one group of people is inferior to or adversely different from another group based on skin color or facial features alone.

I n modern applications of **race**, individuals are grouped together by using visual clues. Skin tone and epicanthic folds (folds of skin that cover the inner corners of the eyes) are often used as racial identifiers. The idea of race is a relatively modern invention. The modern concept of race can be traced to a book by Carl Linnaeus called *Systema*

Naturae (1740) where he said there are four human races: *Homo europaeus, Homo afer, Homo americanus, and Homo asiaticus.* Over the years these races were redefined to just three, with George Cuvier calling them Caucasian, Mongolian, and Negro. But modern scientific research into the human DNA structure shows that there is no scientific evidence of human races or subraces, suggesting a 99.9 percent similarity among all humans from a genetic standpoint. Race has thus manifested itself mainly as a visually based identifier of humans.

For decades, South Africa enforced a strict system of racial segregation called "apartheid." This photo from the 1970s shows a "Europeans only" bench from Johannesburg, South Africa. On the right it says "whites only" in Afrikaans.

Ethnicity is a state of belonging to a cultural group with a common history or cultural system. Ethnicity can be combined with nationality (based on where someone was born or nationalized), or just applied to a cultural group. Typically, race and ethnicity become labels of people, even if there is no genetic reason behind it. A group of people that are outnumbered by another group are called a **minority**. Minorities can be people of a single ethnicity or racial label who are outnumbered by another ethnicity or race. The foundation of both race and ethnicity is the sense of belonging or "other." A simple way to think about this is an idea of "my group" and "their group," or a sense of "us" and "them." The human tendency to group together with like-minded people creates the sense of "other," and race and ethnicity are easy targets for stereotypical classification, because there are visual identifiers to them being "different."

MINORITY RIGHTS VIOLATIONS

All people should have the right to participate in their own cultural lives and communities. If someone is singled out because of race, ethnicity, or just because of how they look, it is a violation of their rights.

People cannot be evicted from their houses, forced to live in substandard areas, or prevented from moving into a neighborhood just because they are part of a minority group. Minorities have the right to health, food, water, and sanitation. They have an equal right to education and education opportunities, and to employment and employment opportunities. These rights cannot be denied to someone just because there is a majority who may not want to allow others to have these rights.

MINORITY TENSION

A *minority group* often defined as a group of people who can be racially or ethnically identified and have a lower population than another group that can be racially or

THE U.S. VOTING RIGHTS ACT OF 1965

President Lyndon Johnson signed the Voting Rights Act on August 6, 1965. The act was designed to overcome barriers to people's right to vote according to the Constitution of the United States. In the early 20th century, several states created barriers to keep African Americans from voting, including poll taxes and voter literacy tests. The Voting Rights Act made it illegal to create laws and voting regulations that were designed to keep or hinder minorities from voting. It also placed rules on states that had previously passed discriminatory laws to need federal approval to change any voting laws in their state. In the case of the Voting Rights Act, it was necessary to create laws specifically keeping the majority from hindering the minority.

President Lyndon Johnson greets civil rights leader Martin Luther King Jr. at the signing of the Voting Rights Act, 1965.

A memorial to those killed in the 1994 genocide, in the Musanze district of Rwanda.

ethnically identified. **Racism** is the idea that one group of people is inferior to or adversely different from another group based on skin color or facial features alone. Ethnic racism occurs when a group of people with a common culture are grouped together and treated as inferior. But, as mentioned earlier, race and ethnicity often get combined, especially if there are visual clues.

Race and racism can lead to racial tensions in which people get divided up by skin color into opposing groups. Many times, racial identity is stronger than ethnicity and cultural history. In extreme cases, ethnic conflict can break out, even to the point of wars. These **ethnic conflicts** are based on differences of ethnicity and culture to the point that one or both of the groups are willing to fight to get rid of the other or to defend their way of life. In extreme cases, ethnic conflict can even develop into **ethnic cleansing**, a policy of trying to get rid of an entire group of people based solely on their ethnicity and differences. In 1915 the Ottoman Empire killed between 800,000 and 1.5 million minority Armenians in an attempt to kill all of the Armenians in the empire, in what is known as the "Great

ORGANIZATION FOR SECURITY AND CO-OPERATION IN EUROPE

The Organization for Security and Co-operation in Europe (OSCE) is an agency that specifically tries to eliminate ethnic tensions by promoting the rights of minorities and identifying areas of concern. The OSCE addresses these issues by supporting fair elections, universal education, gender equality, freedom of the press, human rights, and cultural rights. The agency is intended to address minority issues before they escalate into ethnic conflicts, and to help maintain minority rights. In 2004 the OSCE played a large role in helping Croatia process its war crimes, assisted in the return of refugees, and oversaw the re-establishment of the rule of law, ultimately helping Croatia to enter the European Union in 2013.

Crime." In 1994 in Rwanda, the Hutu majority systematically killed over 100,000 of the minority Tutsi in an effort to get rid of all Tutsis through ethnic cleansing.

When a particular ethnicity is in the minority, life can be very difficult for them. Even if the ethnic tensions are not as extreme as the examples above, minority groups can still face discrimination. It is important for there to be a minority voice in a democratic system. Minority groups should be allowed to exist, and they should be able to let the majority know what they desire.

MINORITY VOICE

Being a minority in a democracy can be inherently problematic, because if there is a cultural difference of opinion, the majority ethnicity will be in full control of government and make all of the decisions. These decisions may neglect the minority or give the majority preferential treatment.

A mural from Saskatoon, Canada, celebrates the diversity of that community.

TRAGEDY OF THE COMMONS

An idea described by William Forster Lloyd of England in 1833 became known as the "Tragedy of the Commons." Lloyd's argument was related to common areas where families were allowed to graze their cows. The common area offered an amount of grass for the cows to eat. Lloyd remarked that shepherds were using the same area to graze their sheep, and that the sheep ate more of the grass than the cows. Cows eat just the tops of the grass, whereas sheep eat all the way to the ground.

Lloyd was concerned that the shepherds were getting a financial benefit from the sheep using the commons, and he noted that if too many sheep were introduced to the common area, it would risk overgrazing. This would ruin the system for everyone, including the cows. He argued that if people are just concerned about their own interests and do nothing about the community at large, the whole community can be adversely affected. This concept became known as the "Tragedy of the Commons."

Lloyd's idea spread beyond the land use of 1833 England. The idea is that we must consider the greater good of all the citizens of our area if we are to succeed as a group. If an individual or majority acts selfishly or is self-serving, it could destroy the system. Therefore we must be cooperative with everyone in the community, even if we have the authority to not cooperate.

One potential problem for the rule of democracy is that a minority voice may not be heard. This can occur because the majority does not think it necessary to address their needs, or because the majority is too busy to think about minorities. If people are operating under a majority-rule government, it can be difficult for minorities and minority populations to get what they want or need. Many societies have attempted to make sure that the majority does not neglect or discriminate against the minority by allowing minority representation and minority responses to majority decisions. It is important to allow people who are different from the majority to voice their concerns and be heard. In Europe the policy of "positive action" is used to help groups not in the majority be represented in the workplace, political positions, and educational institutions. The United States has a similar process called "affirmative action." In both cases, the policies are there to encourage the representation of minorities and try to reduce the possibility of prejudice.

TEXT-DEPENDENT QUESTIONS

1. What is the difference between race and ethnicity?
2. How can minority rights be violated?
3. What can happen if one group tries to get rid of another through violence?

RESEARCH PROJECTS

1. Choose a country you are interested in. Look up the statistics on your country and find out which are the main minority groups. Write an essay on the ways these groups can get their voices heard.
2. How does your country identify different races? Write an essay on how race creates a visual identity that may not be accurate in identifying the individual.

FURTHER READING

BOOKS

Binder, Sarah A. *Minority Rights, Majority Rule: Partisanship and the Development of Congress.* Cambridge: Cambridge University Press, 1997.

Hepple, Bob, and Erika M. Szyszczak, eds. *Discrimination: The Limits of Law.* London: Mansell, 1992.

Hurd, Elizabeth Shakman. *Beyond Religious Freedom: The New Global Politics of Religion.* Princetion, NJ: Princeton University Press, 2015.

Mutua, Makau. *Human Rights: A Political and Cultural Critique.* Philadelphia: University of Pennsylvania Press, 2008.

Nash, Kate. *The Cultural Politics of Human Rights: Comparing the US and UK.* Cambridge: Cambridge University Press, 2009.

Patten, Alan. *Equal Recognition: The Moral Foundations of Minority Rights.* Princeton, NJ: Princeton University Press, 2014.

Skrentny, John D. *The Minority Rights Revolution.* Cambridge, MA: Belknap Press of Harvard University Press, 2002.

Silverman, Helaine, and D. Fairchild Ruggles. *Cultural Heritage and Human Rights.* New York: Springer, 2007.

ONLINE

Amnesty International. https://www.amnesty.org/en/.

International Coalition for Religious Freedom. http://www.religiousfreedom.com/.

United for Human Rights. http://www.humanrights.com/#/home.

United Nations High Commissioner for Refugees. http://www.unhcr.org/cgi-bin/texis/vtx/home.

Universal Declaration of Human Rights. http://www.un.org/en/documents/udhr/.

SERIES GLOSSARY

accountability: making elected officials and government workers answerable to the public for their actions, and holding them responsible for mistakes or crimes.

amnesty: a formal reprieve or pardon for people accused or convicted of committing crimes.

anarchist: a person who believes that government should be abolished because it enslaves or otherwise represses people.

assimilation: the process through which immigrants adopt the cultural, political, and social beliefs of a new nation.

autocracy: a system of government in which a small circle of elites holds most, if not all, political power.

belief: an acceptance of a statement or idea concerning a religion or faith.

citizenship: formal recognition that an individual is a member of a political community.

civil law: statutes and rules that govern private rights and responsibilities and regulate noncriminal disputes over issues such as property or contracts.

civil rights: government-protected liberties afforded to all people in democratic countries.

civil servants: people who work for the government, not including elected officials or members of the military.

corruption: illegal or unethical behavior on the part of officials who abuse their position.

democracy: A government in which the people hold all or most political power and express their preferences on issues through regular voting and elections.

deportation: the legal process whereby undocumented immigrants or those who have violated residency laws are forced to leave their new country.

dual citizenship: being a full citizen of two or more countries.

election: the process of selecting people to serve in public office through voting.

expatriate: someone who resides in a country other than his or her nation of birth.

feminism: the belief in social, economic, and political equality for women.

gender rights: providing access to equal rights for all members of a society regardless of their gender.

glass ceiling: obstacles that prevent the advancement of disadvantaged groups from obtaining senior positions of authority in business, government, and education.

globalization: a trend toward increased interconnectedness between nations and cultures across the world; globalization impacts the spheres of politics, economics, culture, and mass media.

guest workers: citizens of one country who have been granted permission to temporarily work in another nation.

homogenous: a region or nation where most people have the same ethnicity, language, religion, customs, and traditions.

human rights: rights that everyone has, regardless of birthplace or citizenship.

incumbent: an official who currently holds office.

industrialization: the transformation of social life resulting from the technological and economic developments involving factories.

jurisdiction: the official authority to administer justice through activities such as investigations, arrests, and obtaining testimony.

minority: a group that is different—ethnically, racially, culturally, or in terms of religion— within a larger society.

national security: the combined efforts of a country to protect its citizens and interests from harm.

naturalization: the legal process by which a resident noncitizen becomes a citizen of a country.

nongovernmental organization (NGO): a private, nonprofit group that provides services or attempts to influence governments and international organizations.

oligarchy: a country in which political power is held by a small, powerful, but unelected group of leaders.

partisanship: a strong bias or prejudice toward one set of beliefs that often results in an unwillingness to compromise or accept alternative points of view.

refugees: people who are kicked out of their country or forced to flee to another country because they are not welcome or fear for their lives.

right-to-work laws: laws in the United States that forbid making union membership a condition for employment.

secular state: governments that are not officially influenced by religion in making decisions.

sexism: system of beliefs, or ideology, that asserts the inferiority of one sex and justifies discrimination based on gender.

socialist: describes a political system in which major businesses or industries are owned or regulated by the community instead of by individuals or privately owned companies.

socioeconomic status: the position of a person within society, based on the combination of their income, wealth, education, family background, and social standing.

sovereignty: supreme authority over people and geographic space. National governments have sovereignty over their citizens and territory.

theocracy: a system of government in which all major decisions are made under the guidance of religious leaders' interpretation of divine authority.

treason: the betrayal of one's country.

tyranny: rule by a small group or single person.

veto: the ability to reject a law or other measure enacted by a legislature.

wage gap: the disparity in earnings between men and women for their work.

INDEX

INDEX

ABOUT THE AUTHOR

David H. Holt received his Ph.D. from the University of Arkansas at Fayetteville and is currently an associate professor of geography in the department of Geography and Geology at the University of Southern Mississippi. Dr. Holt teaches courses on sustainable development, conservation of natural resources, world regional geography, and cartography. Dr. Holt in an environmental geographer who has raised over $400K in funding with research interests in dendrochronology, migration theory, necrogeography, and post-disaster resilience.

ABOUT THE ADVISOR

Tom Lansford is a Professor of Political Science, and a former academic dean, at the University of Southern Mississippi, Gulf Coast. He is a member of the governing board of the National Social Science Association and a state liaison for Mississippi for Project Vote Smart. His research interests include foreign and security policy, and the U.S. presidency. Dr. Lansford is the author, coauthor, editor or coeditor of more than 40 books, and the author of more than one hundred essays, book chapters, encyclopedic entries, and reviews. Recent sole-authored books include: *A Bitter Harvest: U.S. Foreign Policy and Afghanistan* (2003), the *Historical Dictionary of U.S. Diplomacy Since the Cold War* (2007) and *9/11 and the Wars in Afghanistan and Iraq: A Chronology and Reference Guide* (2011). His more recent edited collections include: *America's War on Terror* (2003; second edition 2009), *Judging Bush* (2009), and *The Obama Presidency: A Preliminary Assessment* (2012). Dr. Lansford has served as the editor of the annual *Political Handbook of the World* since 2012.

PHOTO CREDITS

Cover: iStock.com/Juanmonino; iStock.com/Nikada; Shutterstock/NZGMW
iStock.com: 20 Alexander Gatsenko; 22 summersetretrievers; 30 diverroy; 36 PTW; 37 stu99; 41 Delpixart; 43 Joel Carillet; 52 Robert_Ford
Pixabay: 11 suc; 12 falco; 16 Jeevan; 24 ebrahim; 46 Richgold; 54 Theo_Q
Shutterstock: 14 Arkady Mazor; 34 Chuck Wagner
Wikimedia Commons: 6 Al Jazeera English; 17 Al Jazeera English; 25 Wolfgang Sauber; 27 Rizka; 32 Arrto; 33 Tomas Castelazo; 44 www_ukberri_net; 49 Martinvl; 51 Yoichi Okamoto